Civilian gas-mask drill, Soviet Union

Retronaut

THE PHOTOGRAPHIC TIME MACHINE

CHRIS WILD

![National Geographic logo] NATIONAL GEOGRAPHIC

WASHINGTON, D.C.

Opposite: **1964** Boxing champion Cassius Clay (the future Muhammad Ali) and his winnings

ca 1890s Zebra-Drawn Carriage

Walter Rothschild, second Baron Rothschild of the
Rothschild finance dynasty, and his team of zebras,
Hyde Park, London. Baron Rothschild was a lifelong
zoologist and had his own zoo.

1961 American jazz trumpeter Louis Armstrong serenades his wife and the Sphinx at the Pyramids at Giza, Egypt.

An off-screen laugh on the set of *Star Wars: Return of the Jedi*

Introduction

One Sunday evening in 1978, the eight-year-old me watched the closing credits of *All Creatures Great and Small* with tears streaming down my cheeks. The TV show, based on well-loved novels by James Herriot, tells the story of a veterinarian in Yorkshire, England, in the 1940s. As the theme music came to an end and

> 66 Life can only be understood backwards; but it must be lived forwards."
> — **Søren Kierkegaard**
> *19th-century Danish philosopher*

the English countryside faded from the screen, I was grief-stricken. I wanted to go to that place, but there was no way to get there. Seeing how upset I was, my dad told me we could visit Yorkshire. But it wasn't Yorkshire that I longed to visit; it was those years—and they were locked away forever.

I had a pathological nostalgia. I grieved not only for my own rapidly receding childhood but also for the years, the "pasts," that I would never experience. The past seemed as real to me as the present, as real as another country. But unlike another country, its borders were closed.

My favorite childhood stories were always about time travel, like *The Devil on the Road,* by Robert Westall, and *Tom's Midnight Garden,* by Philippa Pearce. Traveling back through time happened so easily to the characters in those stories. Why couldn't it happen to me? It seemed like an oversight, a technicality. It was as though I was surrounded by exotic and unexplored countries, and a thief had stolen my passport.

1946 Early color photo of American soldiers outside the Bull Hotel in Cambridge, England

I found it 25 years later. On a wet weekday lunch hour, I was browsing in a discount bookshop in a small seaside town in England. I wasn't looking for anything other than shelter from the rain, and, as with every other lunchtime, an escape from the awful sense of still not knowing what I wanted to be when I grew up.

What I found was a book of color photographs of Britain taken during World War II. This was the first time I had seen color photographs of the 1940s and even earlier decades. As I turned the pages, I found it hard to make sense of what I was seeing. These pictures did not look like the past as I understood it. Instead they looked like "now"—my "now," this "now." The color had wiped away the years, just as polish wipes away the tarnish on a ring.

Poring over these pictures felt like the next best thing to time travel. Each page dislocated my sense of when is "now" and when was "then." The images tore tiny holes in my internal map of the past. This tearing was incredibly powerful.

We all have a map of the past inside our heads. It is an amalgam of all the pictures and films we have seen, the history books we have read, and the stories we have heard about what life used to be like. It is similar to the memory of a physical place that we have visited. For each of us, this map is the past.

But I suddenly realized that my map was inaccurate. It was limited, fixed, and static. It depicted the past as an inferior version of the present—a lower resolution version, with less sex appeal, less star quality, little self-awareness, and mostly in black and white.

Over the next six years, I scoured England's thrift stores, museums, and archives looking for old color photographs. Along the way I found other pictures—both in color and black and white—that were just as effective in ripping up my time map: technological prototypes that were way ahead of their time, predictions for the year 2000 imagined in the year 1900, an invitation to the launch of the *Titanic,* Martha Stewart before her empire, the Eiffel Tower half-built. I was discovering a new brilliantly colorful past of high resolution, high contrast, low noise—and lots and lots of detail.

Finally it dawned on me: No one has ever lived in "the past." Everyone has always lived in "now." What I mean is that being alive in the past felt the same as being alive now. Think of your own life five years ago. What did it feel like? Maybe your hair was longer or shorter, or you had more or less money, but what did it *feel* like to be alive? It felt like "now"—it was just a different version of today.

Why does this matter? It transforms the span of history into a series of drafts of the present. Those early color pictures show that people a hundred years ago were just like us. And the world they built is a resource for us to use, today, in the world we are building.

In January 2010, I started a blog to share the pictures that had changed my life. I chose the name "Retronaut" to mean "someone who travels back." I picked a new pair of old goggles as my logo because a) they are both old and new at the same time and b) because *Retronaut* is about seeing the past through different lenses.

Much to my surprise, these photographs had a contagious effect. Today I am some-what startled to have more than a million people enjoy Retronaut every month.

Now, in my first book, I invite you to travel in my photographic time machine. You'll see the past like you've never seen it before.

CHAPTER ONE

Future

Worlds

1

Time as Potential

Where is the future? Because most of us walk forward, we imagine the future in front of us, over the next horizon — a promise to gain, a prize to attain, our Shangri-la. Politicians will offer a brighter future, fair for all. We see it — almost — as we squint into the setting sun.

> 66 People ask me to predict the future, when all I want to do is prevent it. Better yet, build it."
> — **Ray Bradbury**
> *author of* Fahrenheit 451

Yet it doesn't arrive, because it doesn't exist. The future isn't an actual place, it's just another version of "now," where we imagine technology is shinier, we are happier, and the truly sophisticated smoke electronic cigarettes.

Like heat haze on a desert road, the future hovers on the horizon as a shimmering silver vision of jet packs and sky cars. When we reach it, it has gone — materializing into the everyday reality of "now." Electronic cigarettes are sold cheap at gas stations, and we've long ceased to wonder at their presence.

And so tomorrow arrives, as mundane as today — but also as inspiring. The answer to the question "When?" is always "Now!"

And the shiny technology? It's there. It's still there. It has always been there, waiting for us to find it. Consider this: A thousand years ago, when Vikings landed on what would one day be the U.S.A., they were bombarded by x-rays, radio waves, and infrared light. They just didn't know they were there.

Someday, in the comfort of your home, you'll be able to shop and bank electronically, read instantly updated newswires, analyze the performance of a stock that interests you, send electronic mail across the country, then play Bridge with three strangers in LA, Chicago and Dallas.

Welcome to someday.

Someday is today with the CompuServe Information Service. CompuServe is available through a local phone call in most major U.S. cities. It connects almost any brand or type of personal computer or terminal with our big mainframe computers and data bases. All you need to get started is an inexpensive telephone coupler and easy-to-use software.

CompuServe's basic service costs only $5.00 per hour, billed in minute increments to your charge card.

The CompuServe Information Service is available at many computer stores across the country. Check with your favorite computer center or contact CompuServe.

Welcome to someday

CompuServe

Information Service Division, 5000 Arlington Centre Blvd.
Columbus, Ohio 43220 (614) 457-8650

An H&R Block Company

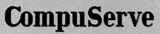

1982 Prophetic CompuServe ad

Conceptual Driving

Experiments in getting from A to B

President Lyndon B. Johnson's Amphicar

One of former U.S. President Johnson's favorite pranks was to drive guests around his Texas ranch in his Amphicar—which could drive on land and in the water. Yelling that the brakes had failed, he would speed downhill and "crash" into his lake—where the car promptly converted into a boat.

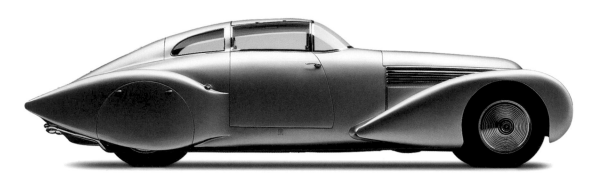

1938 The Hispano-Suiza Dubonnet Xenia

ca 1957 Three-wheeled Messerschmitt KR 201

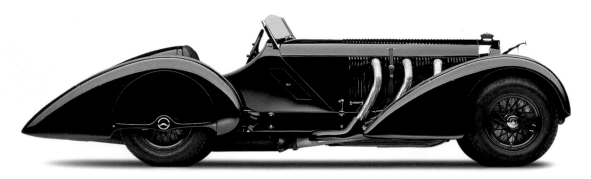

1930 Mercedes-Benz SSK "Count Trossi"

1983 Vespa scooter with a few additional mirrors

1920s A shoe-shaped delivery truck promoting Peters Brothers Shoe Company

1934 Life Savers peppermints promotional car

1970s Ferrari
Modulo Concept Car

The visual godparent of James Bond's white Lotus Esprit in the movie *The Spy Who Loved Me,* the Ferrari Modulo was painted black when it first zoomed onto the public stage. Later the vehicle was re-released in white. The razor-thin, lustworthy race car won multiple design awards but was never a production model.

1980s Digital Dashboards

Clockwise from left to right: Lancia Orca
by ItalDesign; Pontiac Trans Am GTA;
Chevrolet Corvette; Citroën BX "Digit"

> **❝** I am the voice of Knight Industries Two Thousand's microprocessor, K.I.T.T. KITT if you prefer."
>
> **— K.I.T.T.**
>
> *the invincible talking car from 1980s TV show* Knight Rider

Late 1940s Winged Automobile

The Aerocar flies and drives on land. Concerned your wingspan may be too wide for winding country roads? No problem. Simply fold back the detachable wings and tow them in a trailer.

1930s Monocycles

The electric Dynasphere (left) and
Motorwheel (right) look just as brilliantly
sci-fi now as they did in the 1930s.

They Were the Robots

Automatons and other early mechanical creatures

1808 Tippu's Tiger

This life-size automaton enshrined a rivalry between Tippu Sultan, ruler of the Indian kingdom of Mysore, and the British East India Company—which ultimately would bring about the end of Tippu's kingdom. Turning the handle launches a sequence of mechanical movements that make the Indian tiger growl and the British man howl. Tippu's Tiger also contains a fully operational organ, constructed with extreme precision.

1959 Robot Band

This band of electrically controlled musicians performed at the Robot Club in Lens, France. Their facial expressions automatically changed to fit the music they played. The machines stood up to play and sat down when they finished.

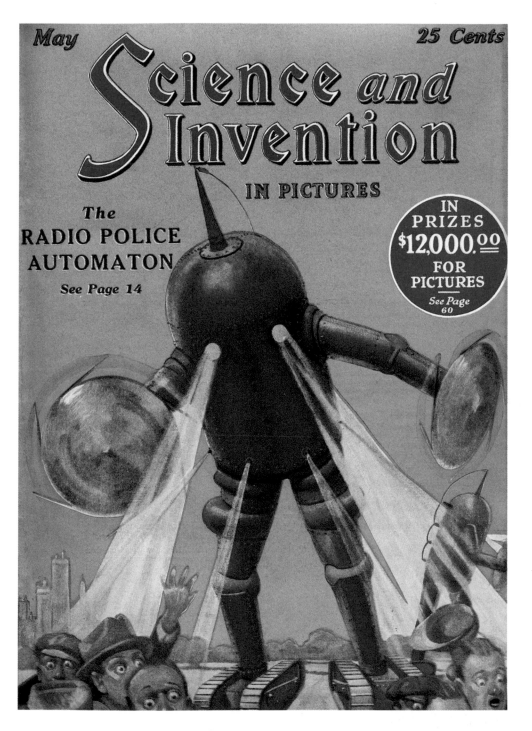

1924 The Radio Police Automaton could be the future of policing.

1974 Jaws, aka "Bruce"

One of three robotic fear machines from Steven Spielberg's aquatic thriller *Jaws,* this 25-foot (8 m) shark is at least 5 feet (2 m) longer than a real great white. Controlled by pneumatic hoses, the sharks regularly malfunctioned and were largely responsible for the film's skyrocketing budget. Why "Bruce"? The sharks are named after Bruce Ramer, Spielberg's lawyer.

1871 The Creepy Creeping Doll

With the original patent tag still attached to its leg, this invention demonstrates an advance in the mechanical crawling doll. George Pemberton Clarke named his creation "Natural Creeping Baby Doll." The arms and legs are hinged to a clockwork body and imitate a crawling motion, but the robot doll actually moves forward by rolling on two toothed wheels.

> *I visualize a time when we will be to robots what dogs are to humans, and I'm rooting for the machines."*
>
> **— Claude Shannon**
> *20th-century American engineer*

2002 A wolf and a Maltese are curious about Aibo, the robot dog.

ca 1820 Jeweled Caterpillar

Attributed to Swiss watchmaker Henri Maillardet, this pearl, enamel, and gold-adorned insect has clockwork cogs that make the lifelike caterpillar crawl. As the front of the caterpillar lifts, the rest of the body follows suit, propelling it forward. Maillardet gave his creature an exotic name, "The Ethiopian Caterpillar," and brought it to London hoping to sell it to visiting Chinese aristocracy.

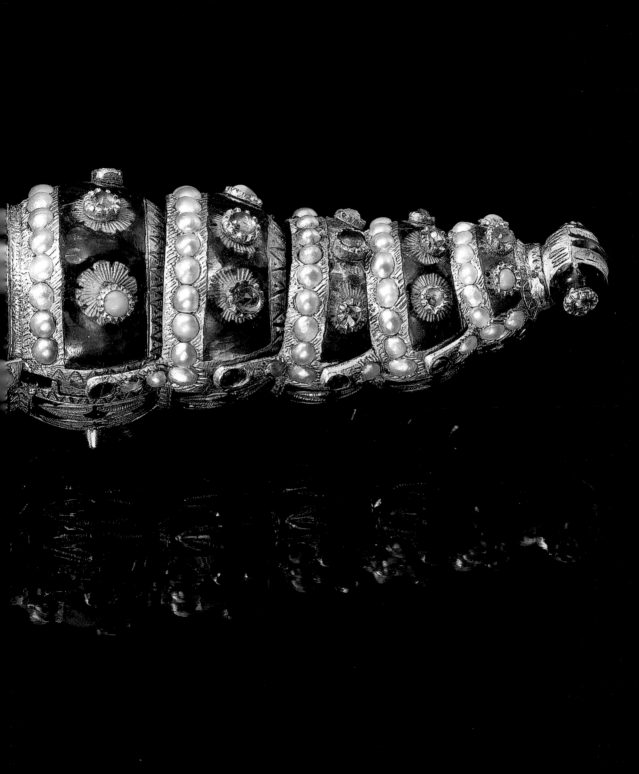

1560 Monk Automaton

Parading in a square, this kinetic monk beats its chest in penitence, lifts a cross toward the heavens, nods its head, and rolls its eyes—all while shaping silent prayers with its lips and pausing only to kiss the cross. According to legend, Spanish King Philip II had beseeched God for a miracle at the bedside of his gravely ill son and promised to supply a miracle in return. His son recovered, and Philip made good on his promise by having this automated monk constructed.

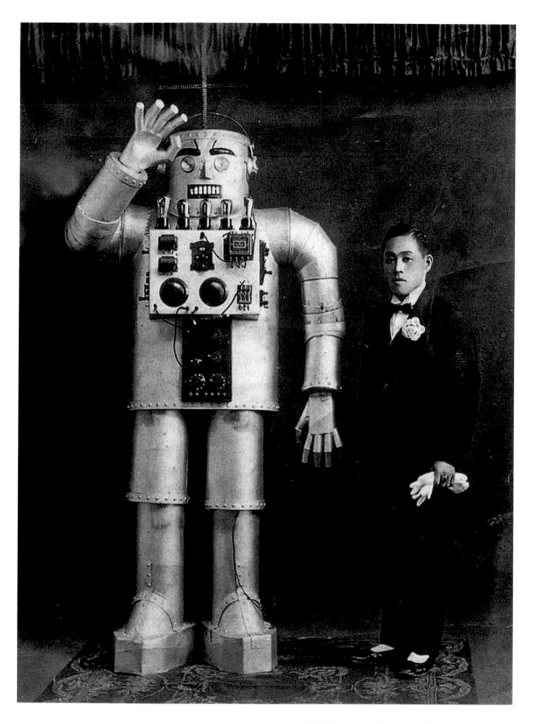

1932 Yasutaro Mitsui and his steel humanoid

Small Steps
for Mankind

Going into orbit through trial and error

Practicing the Moonwalk

A special harness helps simulate the experience
of living in a low-gravity environment.

> " A rocket will never be able to leave the Earth's atmosphere."
> — *New York Times*
> **January 13, 1920**
>
> *The* Times *offered a retraction on July 17, 1969, as Apollo 11 traveled to the moon.*

1966 Splashdown Training

If you have ever fallen out of Earth's atmosphere in a cramped metal container at massive acceleration and landed with impact in the ocean, you'll know that getting out of the door is not entirely straightforward. Apollo 1 astronauts Edward H. White, Roger B. Chaffee, and Virgil I. Grissom practice this maneuver in a swimming pool at Ellington Field Air Force Base near Houston, Texas. Tragically, it was never required. All three were killed in a fire in their command module during a launch rehearsal.

ПОКОРИМ
КОСМОС!

С праздником
ВЕЛИКОГО
ОКТЯБРЯ

ca 1960 Interstellar Propaganda

Soviet posters celebrate the space race. Left: "Let's Conquer Space!" in Russian. Above: A poster celebrating the anniversary of the Russian Revolution of October 1917 shows rockets, Sputniks, and other Soviet spacecraft.

1977 AX-3 Pressure Suit

The AX-3 was a prototype space suit designed by
NASA to allow for ease of mobility while providing
a constant internal pressure. The suit also
boasted a fishbowl helmet and red accents.

1960 Belka (left) and Strelka back on Earth after a successful orbital flight

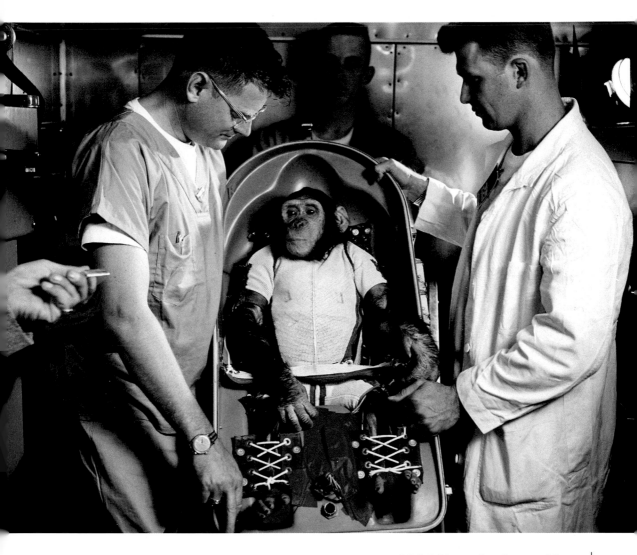

1961 Ham the Astrochimp

Ham was three years old when he made his suborbital voyage. Inside his rocket, Ham launched out of Earth's atmosphere, traveling 157 miles (253 km) above Earth. Ham had one mission: When a light flashed, his job was to pull the correct lever. He performed the task well and returned to Earth safely and in good health.

1976 The crew of *Star Trek*'s *Enterprise* at the dedication of the space shuttle *Enterprise*

1960s NASA's Model Space Modules

NASA tackles the most critical question of the entire space program: What will the ship look like? Left: A 1963 prototype for the Apollo Lunar Lander, called a "bug." Right: A model of a biosatellite capsule sent into space in 1969 with a chimp in front and a life support package in the back.

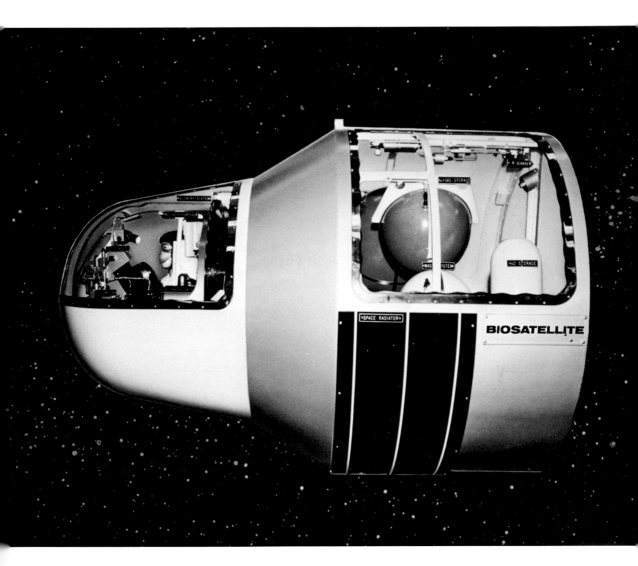

Remembering Tomorrow

The future as seen from the past

1926 London in 2026

The text that accompanied this 1926 poster read, "London 2026 A.D.—This is all in the air. Today—the solid comfort of the Underground." This vision of the way the new technology might change transportation in London predicts, relatively accurately, the size and number of skyscrapers that are now being built in central London, dwarfing St. Paul's Cathedral (the small dome in the middle of the poster).

Early 1900s Listening Devices

In essence, an enhanced version of the cupped hand, these devices were rendered obsolete with the arrival of radar. Left: Listening device at a Berlin air defense unit (1939). Right: A WWI French soldier with an acoustic device capable of tracking airplanes (ca 1914).

1902 Women of the Future

A set of playing cards produced by the French postcard manufacturer Albert Bergeret envision the careers available to women of the future. (Top row, left to right): painter, infantry soldier, lawyer, second lieutenant, politician, rural guard. (Middle row, left to right): jockey, journalist, mayor, marine, master of weaponry. (Bottom row, left to right): doctor, firefighter, drummer.

Les Femmes de l'Avenir

9. - Sous-Lieutenant

Les Femmes de l'Avenir

2. - Garde Champêtre

Les Femmes de l'Avenir
19. - Maire

Les Femmes de l'Avenir

7. - Marin

Les Femmes de l'Avenir

14. - Maître-d'Armes

Les Femmes de l'Avenir

4. - Pompier

Les Femmes de l'Avenir

5. - Petit Tambour

Mail letters over the phone!

The amazing Xerox Magnafax Telecopier
can send an exact copy anywhere in the country.
Over ordinary telephone equipment.

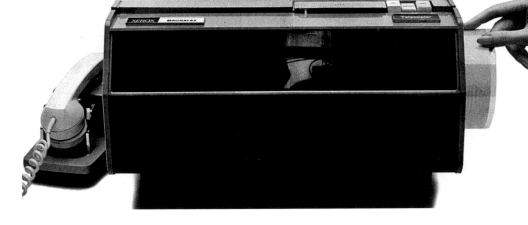

1966 Xerox Magnafax Telecopier ad

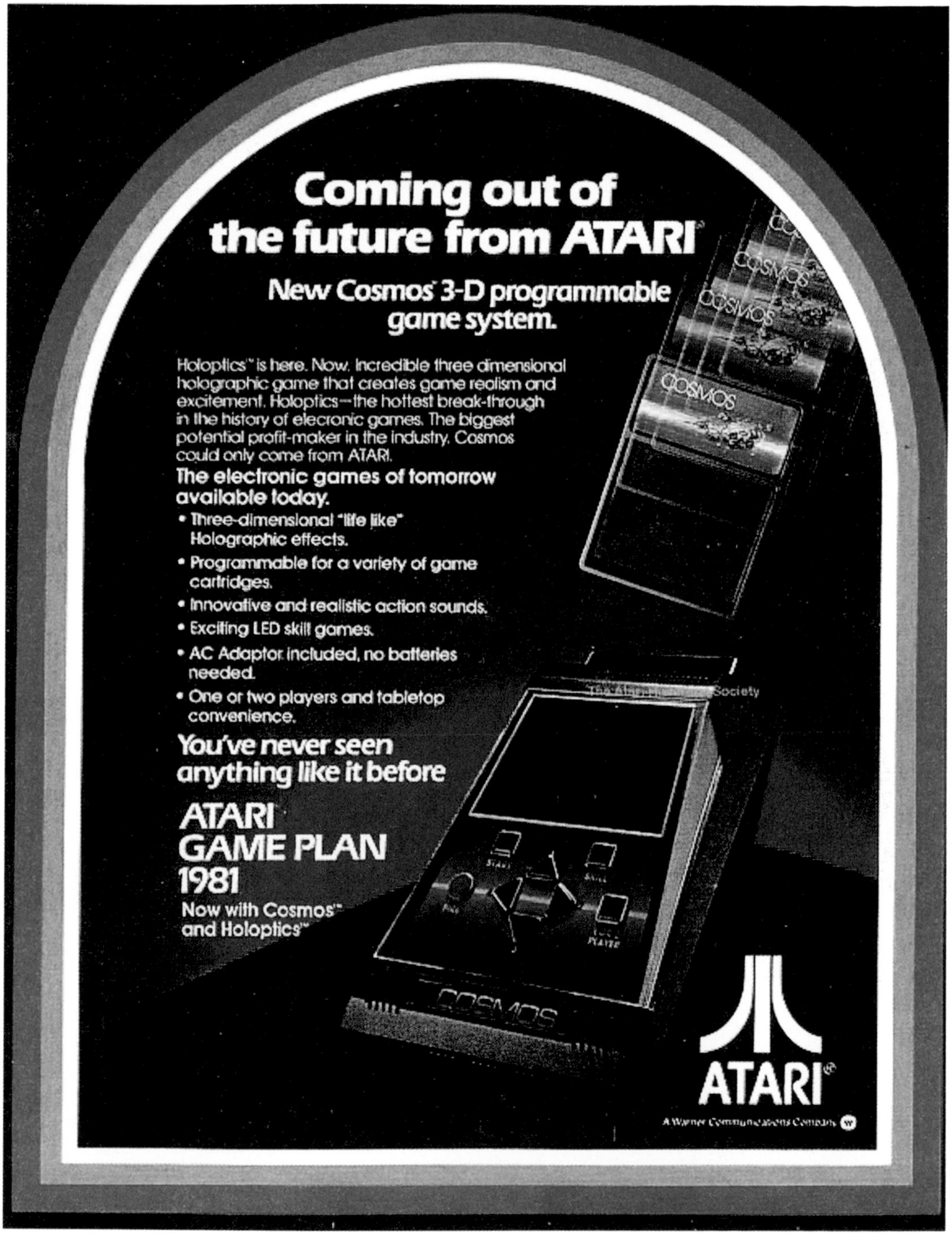

1981 Atari Game Plan console ad

1970 World's Fair, Osaka, Japan

The Toshiba IHI Pavilion housed a nine-screen cinema and a revolving floor that could be raised and lowered. In the year 6970, you—or, rather, your descendants—may witness the opening of the 5,000-year time capsule buried on the site of Expo '70. Another time capsule is scheduled to be opened every 100 years at the turn of the century, and was opened for the first time in 2000.

1950s Shopping Online

The toast lying cold on the work surface, this woman is hypnotized (as we are today) by shopping from a screen, and also by a spokesmodel who looks eerily like herself.

Hildebrands Deutscher Kakao
Hildebrands Deutsche Schokolade
Bewegliche Trottoire im Jahre 2000.

Hildebrands Deutsche Schokolade
Bewegliche Häuser im Jahre 2000.

Hildebrands Deutscher Kakao
Theater im Jahre 2000.

Hildebrands Deutsche Schokolade
Flugmaschine im Jahre 2000.

Hildebrands Deutsche Schokolade
Schönwettermaschine im Jahre 2000.

Hildebrands Deutsche Schokolade
Schiffseisenbahn im Jahre 2000.

Hildebrands Deutsche Schokolade
Unterseeische Schiffe im Jahre 2000.

Hildebrands Deutscher Kakao
Ueberdachte Stadt im Jahre 2000.

ca 1900 In the Year 2000

These German postcards imagine the year 2000 from the vantage point of the year 1900. (Top row, left to right): moving pavement, home-moving by train, a quick stroll on the water. (Second row, left to right): theater, personal flying machines. (Third row, left to right): weather control machine, combined ship and railway locomotive, personal airships, summer holidays at the North Pole. (Bottom row, left to right): undersea tourist boats, roofed cities, police x-ray surveillance.

CHAPTER TWO

Icons U

nmade

2

Time as Equalizer

We all exist as one thing, and that thing has a name: "humanity." We are all human and only human. Those stars we adore—they aren't stars, but reflectors that shine our own light back to us. The monuments we revere were created by us. So if someone or something is sitting up on a pedestal, guess who placed it there? You and I did.

> 66 My own motto is: When you're through changing, you're through."
> —**Martha Stewart**

In this chapter, you'll see Princess Diana as an awkward 19-year-old girl, before she wore a crown. Marilyn Monroe started out as Norma Jeane, and a nondescript mountain became Mount Rushmore. The Statue of Liberty arrived in the United States in pieces awaiting assembly, and is now a symbol of freedom to people all over the world.

When we brush away the stardust and see our stars as people, or our iconic buildings as construction sites of stone and metal and concrete, we see our own opportunities revealed. We, too, are made of raw materials. And the finished product is so much more than the sum of the parts.

As Oscar Wilde reportedly said at New York Customs Control in 1882, "I have nothing to declare but my genius." You can declare yours whenever you like.

The world is waiting.

Early 1960s Martha Stewart, fashion model

Superstars
Starting Out

Celebrity in embryonic form

1962 **The Beatles With Gene Vincent**

The fledgling Beatles—minus Ringo—with rockabilly legend
Gene Vincent (left) at the Star-Club, in Hamburg, Germany

1943 Paul Newman enlisting for the Navy

ca 1948 Future Hollywood legend James Dean on the Fairmont, Indiana, basketball team

ca 1972 Bill Clinton and Hillary Rodham at Yale

"She was in my face from the start," said the former U.S. president. "He was the first man I'd met who wasn't afraid of me," said the former secretary of state.

CAST

Don Corleone: Marlon Brando
  John Marley   Laurance Olivier
#850 Carlo Ponti *   *FRANK DE KOVA

Michael Corleone: * AL PACINO
                   * Scott Marlowe
Robert d. Niro   MIKE MARGOTA
Ant. Genovese   (Richard Romanos)
~~Dustin Huffman~~   JIMMY CAAN
25 Mike Parts   ~~MARTIN SHEEN~~

      SONNY CORLEONE:

                   * JIMMY CAAN
20 TONY LO BIANCO CARMINE CARIDI
    ~~PETER FALK~~   * SCOTT MARLOWE
    AL Lettieri   * DON GORDON
                   * (TONY ZERBE)
                      LOU ANTONIO
                   (Paul ~~Shanter~~)
                      Robert Viharo
                   (RUDY SOLARI)
                   JOHN SAXON
                   JOHN BRASCIA
                   Johnny Sette ⑦
    HARRY GUARDINO ADAM ROAKE
                   BEN GAZZARA
25 TOM HAGEN!   * BEN PIAZZA
                   ROBERT DuVall
                   TONY ~~zebe~~
                   * PETER DONAT

ca 1970 Francis Ford Coppola's potential cast list for *The Godfather*

> "People love talking about when they were young and heard 'Honky Tonk Women' for the first time. It's quite a heavy load to carry on your shoulders, the memories of so many people."
>
> — **Mick Jagger**

MICK JAGGER FORMS GROUP

MICK Jagger, R&B vocalist, is taking a rhythm and blues group into the Marquee tomorrow night (Thurs) while Blues Inc. is doing its Jazz Club gig.

Called 'The Rolling Stones' ("I hope they don't think we're a rock 'n' roll outfit", says Mick) the lineup is: Jagger, (voc), Keith Richards, Elmo Lewis (gtrs), Dick Taylor (bass), 'Stu' (pno), Mike Avery (drs).

A second group under Long John Baldry will also be there.

1962 Announcement in *Jazz News* about Mick Jagger's new group

1987 Nicole Kidman

1986 Halle Berry competes in the Miss World beauty contest.

1940 Ronald Reagan, future U.S. president, poses as a model for a sculpture class.

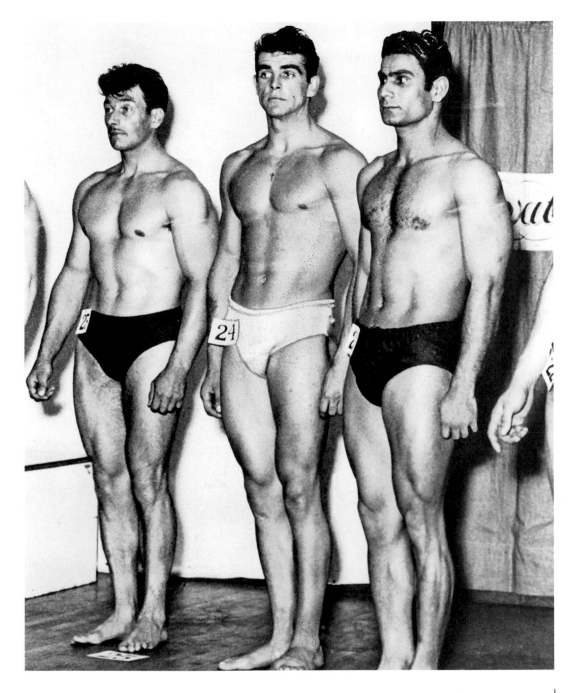

1950 Universe, Meet Mr. Universe

Long before he becomes 007, Sean Connery (white trunks) places third in the Mr. Universe contest.

1947 Norma Jeane begins her transformation into Marilyn Monroe.

1893 Lawyer Mahatma Gandhi

1895 Winston Churchill in the British cavalry

1882 Albert Einstein at three years old

ca 1992 Victoria Beckham (née Adams) pre–Spice Girls pop music stardom

Construction of the Familiar

Bricks and mortar and building blocks of greatness

1930 **The Waldorf Astoria**

Two waiters serve lunch to steelworkers
building the famous New York City hotel.

ca 1935 George Washington's face emerges from the rock, Mount Rushmore, South Dakota

1932 The skeleton of the U.S.S. *Macon,* a flying aircraft carrier

ca 1933 Dignitaries ride over Hoover Dam in a 30-foot-wide (9-m) section of pipe.

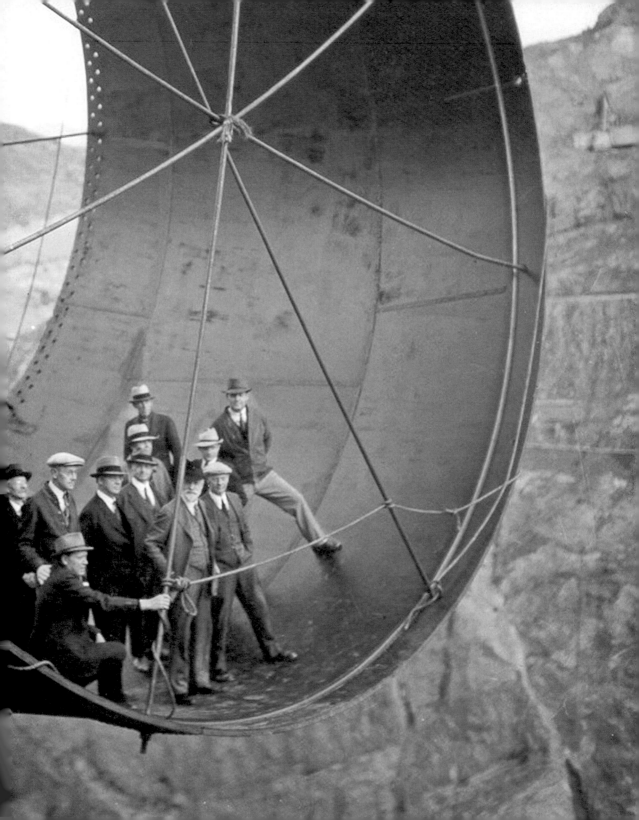

ca 1886 Creating Neuschwanstein Castle in the Bavarian Alps

ca **1954** Creating Disneyland's Sleeping Beauty Castle in California, modeled after Neuschwanstein

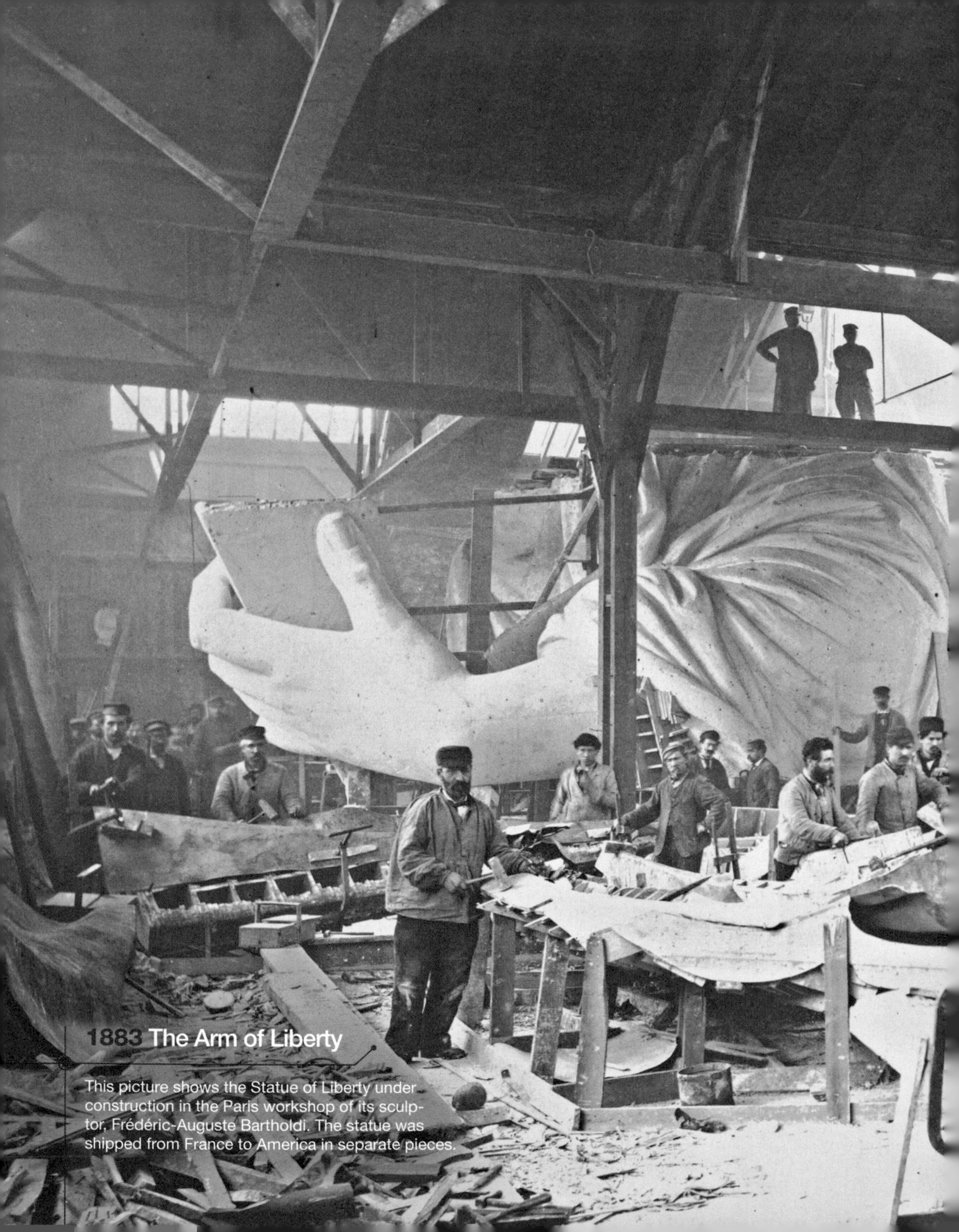

1883 The Arm of Liberty

This picture shows the Statue of Liberty under construction in the Paris workshop of its sculptor, Frédéric-Auguste Bartholdi. The statue was shipped from France to America in separate pieces.

America is an adorable woman chewing tobacco."
— **Frédéric-Auguste Bartholdi**
designer of the Statue of Liberty

1880s Erecting the Eiffel Tower

Gustave Eiffel constructed two of the
world's most iconic structures on two
separate continents—the Eiffel Tower
and, at Bartholdi's request, the internal
structure of the Statue of Liberty.

ca 1911 **The *Titanic***

Originally photographed in black and
white, this image of the *Titanic* under
construction was colorized later.

> " I shall never say again that 13 is an unlucky number. Boat 13 is the best friend we ever had."
> — **Lawrence Beesley**
> *Titanic survivor rescued by Boat 13*

Under the Crown

Regal names, regular people

1917 **The Romanov Children With Measles**

From left to right: Anastasia, Olga, Alexei, Maria, and Tatiana, with heads shaved

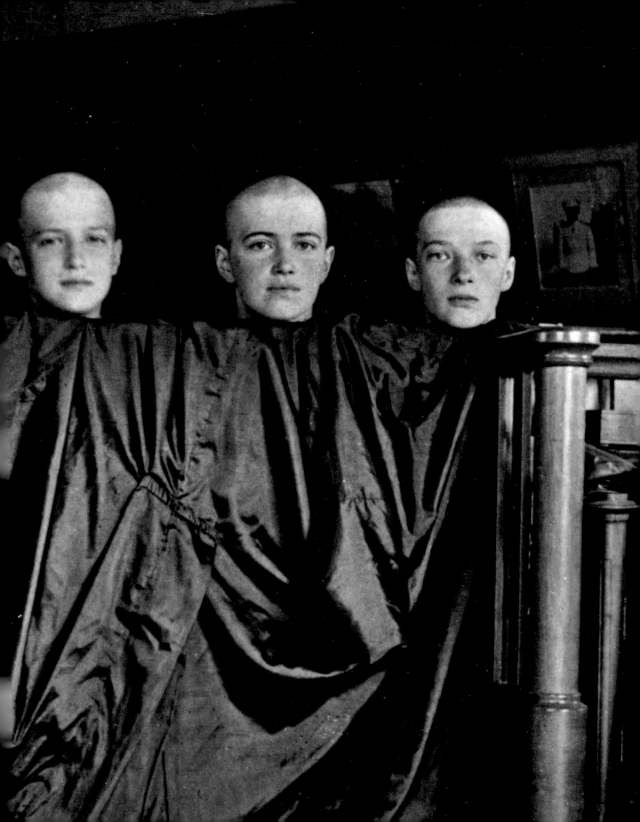

1945 The Queen in the Army

England's Princess Elizabeth wore down her father, King George VI, with persistent requests, until he allowed her to join the war effort. Elizabeth, aka Second Subaltern Elizabeth Windsor (now Queen Elizabeth II), became trained as a mechanic and truck driver.

Early 1910s Anastasia's Selfie

Thirteen-year-old Russian Grand Duchess Anastasia
Nikolaevna sent this self-portrait to a friend with a letter.
She wrote, "I took this picture of myself looking at the
mirror. It was very hard as my hands were trembling."
Self-portraits, or "selfies," have existed since art began.
But this one was taken by an awkward teenager, which
makes it strikingly contemporary.

1917 The Tsar Shovels Snow

Tsar Nicholas II in the park at Tsarskoe Selo, where he and his family were interned at their residence, Alexander Palace

1980 A 19-year-old Diana Spencer stalls her new Mini Metro.

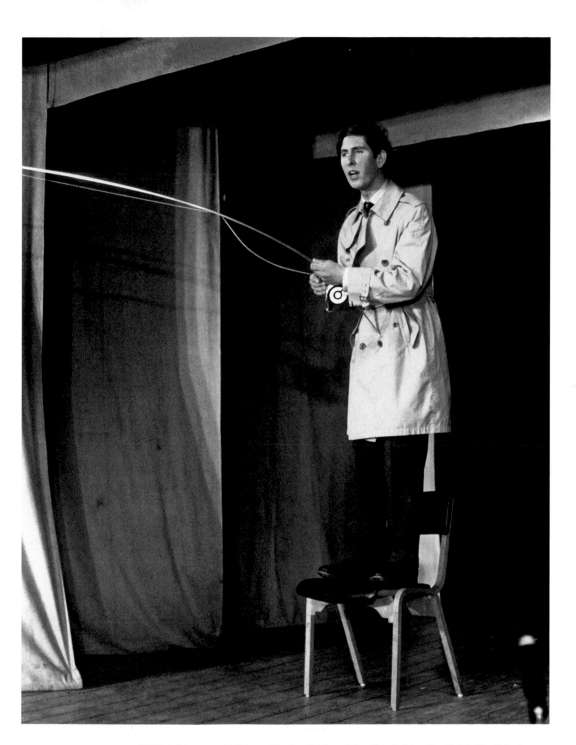

1970 A 21-year-old Prince Charles fishing at the Cambridge Footlights theatrical revue

A Galaxy Not So Far Away

Making movie magic in a workaday world

A Pipe and Plywood *Millennium Falcon*

Star Wars creator George Lucas's design for the *Millennium Falcon* was inspired by a hamburger with an olive as the cockpit. This model was designed for *The Empire Strikes Back*.

1938 "Frankenstein" (Boris Karloff) at his birthday party on the set of the film *Son of Frankenstein*

1953 Dressing the monstrous star of the horror film *Creature from the Black Lagoon*

> 66 The water was filthy, dirt blew into it, and actors splashing around in it got kidney infections, but at least it was heated to 72 degrees."
> — **Kate Winslet**
> *on filming* Titanic

ca 1996 On the Set of *Titanic*

James Cameron directing actors Kate Winslet and Leonardo DiCaprio. During casting, Kate Winslet was never asked whether she could swim. Luckily, she can.

1974 Chain mail–clad actors John Cleese and Graham Chapman on the set of *Monty Python and the Holy Grail*

1961 A chain mail–clad Charlton Heston on the set of the epic film *El Cid*

1967 Dr. Zaius (Maurice Evans) reads the *Daily Mail* during a break in filming *Planet of the Apes*.

ca 1978 Manis the orangutan on the set of *Every Which Way but Loose*

ca 1976 King Kong's Head
at the World Trade Center

Italian movie producer Agostino De
Laurentiis told *Time* magazine:
"No one cry when Jaws die. But when
the monkey die, people gonna cry."

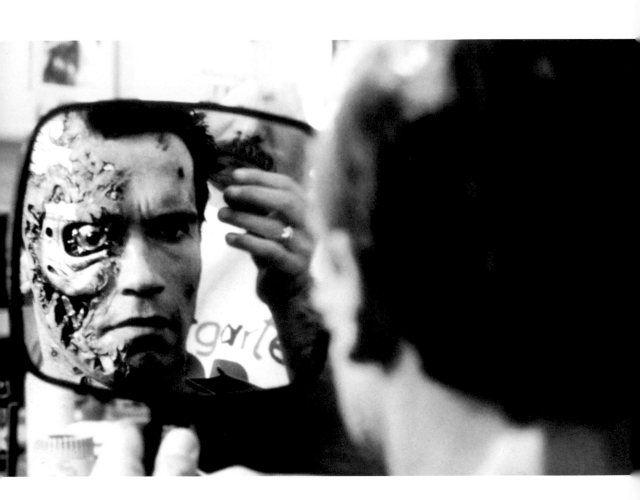

ca 1991 *Terminator 2*

Future California governor Arnold
Schwarzenegger transforms into a
cyborg on the set of *Terminator 2:
Judgment Day.* Eleven million of his
$15 million fee for the movie was
paid in the form of a Gulfstream G-III jet.

1964 Actress Shirley Eaton becomes James Bond's golden girl du jour for the movie *Goldfinger.*

ca 1978 Inside the Alien

The towering creature of *Alien* sci-fi movie fame
was actually an Earthling: seven-foot-two (218 cm)
Nigerian actor Bolaji Badejo.

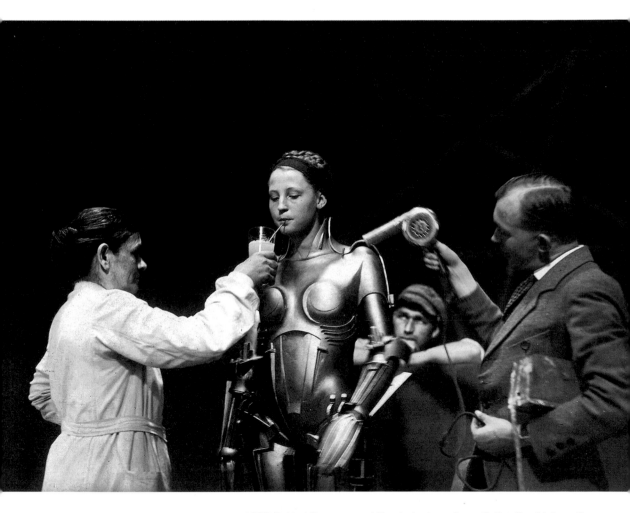

ca **1926** Behind the scenes of the dystopian science fiction film *Metropolis*

> "Even from eight or nine years old, I thought, well, I'll be the greatest rock star in England. I just made up my mind."
> — **David Bowie**

ca 1983 David Bowie's Head

Major Jack Celliers (David Bowie) has been sentenced to death by burying in the movie *Merry Christmas, Mr. Lawrence.* The film is set in a Japanese prisoner of war camp during WWII, but Bowie's hair gel places him firmly in the 1980s.

CHAPTER THREE

The Power

of the Trivial

Time as Detail

Each of us has a map of the past in our head. We have been stitching it together all our lives, but vast areas of our maps are sketchy. We try to sum up the 1920s in one word, "roaring," and the 1960s in another, "groovy." And we see many of our yesterdays in black and white. The past has been smoothed over and washed out, like a faded photograph in sepia.

Enter the detail. Here is a secret message inside Abraham Lincoln's pocket watch. Here is the exact color of George Washington's false teeth. Here is Elvis's library card (he borrowed *The Courageous Heart*).

Enter the laughs. A 19th-century soldier photobombs a formal military portrait. Urban legends go "viral" long before the Internet. And famous novelist Marcel Proust plays air guitar in 1891.

And enter the trivial. An invitation for a Turkish bath on board the Titanic. A 20-sided die used to play an ancient Egyptian game. And people from past generations who strolled along the very same streets we walk on today.

The devil is in the details. So is the eternal.

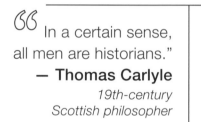

" In a certain sense, all men are historians."

— Thomas Carlyle
19th-century Scottish philosopher

1960 New York street

1954 Waiters' Race in Paris

A French *garçon* (waiter) sprints down a Parisian street balancing beverages on a tray as part of La Course Des Garçons de Café, or The Waiters' Race. Competitions like this still takes place today.

1911 The Auteuil Races

Fashions worn at the steeplechases,
Auteuil Hippodrome, Paris

1966 Motorcycle club members, London

GOING OUT OF WOMAN

（行發館洋東田織）（三風韓）出外の人婦壌平（俗風國韓）

ca 1904 Street Fashions

Above: Korean women
Right: Korean men

66 Fashion's not about looking back. It's always about looking forward."
— **Anna Wintour**
editor in chief of Vogue

1980s On the London Underground

Scenes captured on camera during a photographer's
daily commute to work

1930 Leaping the puddle

1906 Dutch Girls

These young women in Westkapelle, Netherlands, wear the Dutch national dress of the time.

A phone call

Saul Leiter (1923–2013) photographed fragments of New York in bright color—a man ahead of his time.

Rare Survivors

Objects that slipped through time

Left to right: Death mask of composer Felix
Mendelssohn (1809–1847); death mask of writer
Walt Whitman (1819–1892); life mask of writer Johann
Wolfgang von Goethe (1749–1832); death mask of
artist Dante Gabriel Rossetti (1828–1882)

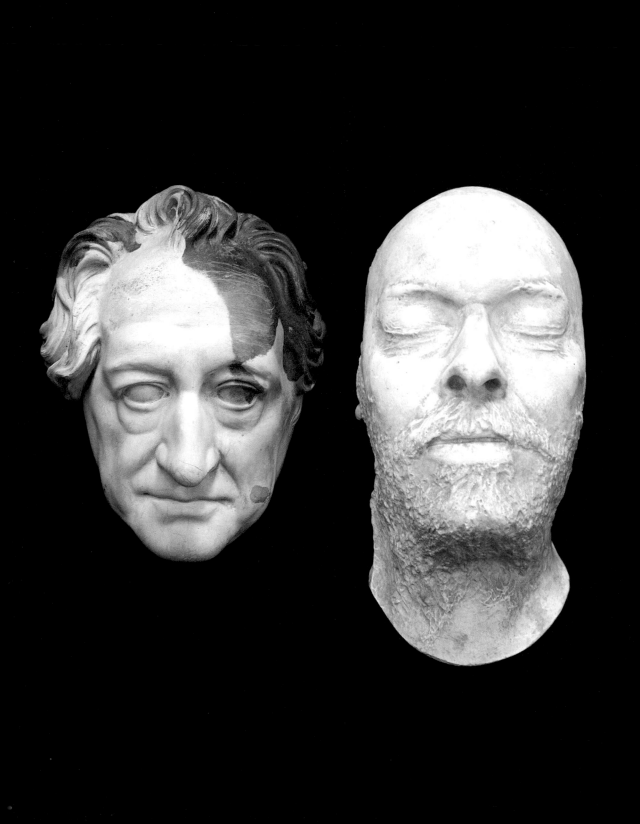

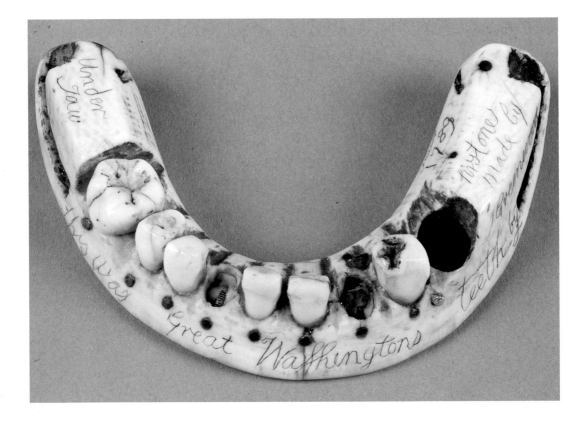

1789 George Washington's Teeth

From a time when false teeth were designed to emulate the condition of the teeth that they replaced, the base of the lower half, shown here, was carved from hippo ivory. The teeth were actually made from human teeth. Washington's mouth had one remaining functioning tooth, hence the hole. This tooth also was later removed from the presidential jaw.

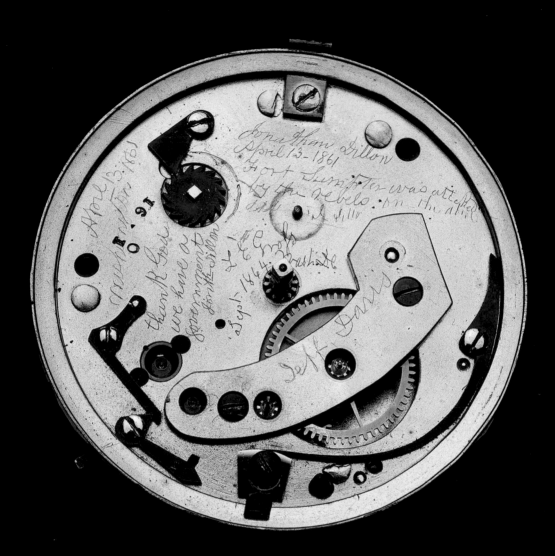

**The Secret Message in
Abraham Lincoln's Pocket Watch**

Watchmaker Jonathan Dillon was repairing Lincoln's pocket watch
when the first shots of the U.S. Civil War were fired. Dillon engraved
a slightly inaccurate message behind the watch's dial: "April 13–1861
Fort Sumpter was attacked by the rebels on the above date J Dillon"
and "thank God we have a government Jonth Dillon." In reality,
Fort Sumter (spelled without a *p*) was attacked on April 12, 1861.
Lincoln never saw the message. It was discovered in 2009 at the
Smithsonian, where the watch is stored, after a tip-off from the great-
great-grandson of Jonathan Dillon.

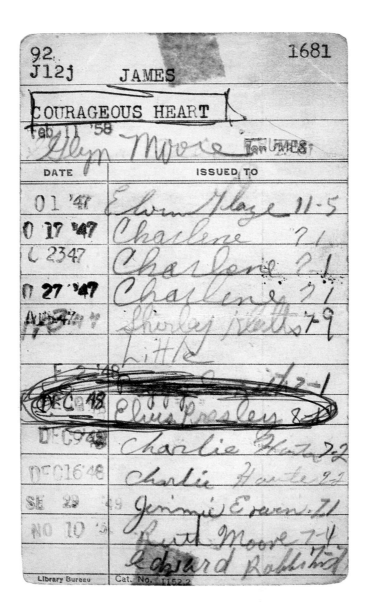

1948 Thirteen-year-old Elvis Presley checks out *The Courageous Heart* from the library.

100s B.C.–A.D. 300s An Egyptian 20-sided die

Launch

OF

White Star Royal Mail Triple-Screw Steamer

"TITANIC"

At BELFAST,

Wednesday, 31st May, 1911, at 12-15 p.m.

Admit Bearer.

1912 *Titanic* Artifacts

Clockwise from top left: Stewards' badges; an envelope addressed to 3rd Officer H. J. Pittman, along with his brass Thunderer whistle; a Turkish bath ticket; an invitation to the *Titanic*'s launch in Belfast, Ireland

Mr H. J. Pittman
Third officer of the Titanic
Washington D.C.
(Continental Hotel)
U.S. POSTAGE
TWO CENTS
No. 659
WHITE STAR LINE.
R.M.S. "TITANIC."
This ticket entitles bearer to use of Turkish or Electric Bath on one occasion.
Paid 4/- or 1 Dollar.
MY WHISTLE SAVED FROM THE S.S. TITANIC APRIL 1912
H. J. Pittman. 3rd mate
9th Nov: 1945 To Ted

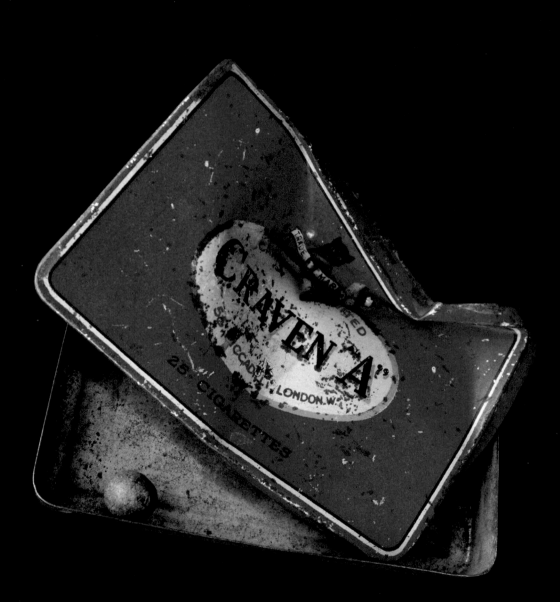

1914 **Lifesaving Cigarette Tin**

British army pilot Arthur Mann carried this cigarette tin in his pocket on the day he was shot. The bullet bounced off the tin and saved his life. (The musket ball shown here for scale is not the actual bullet.)

"Above all else, guard your heart for it affects everything else you do."
— Proverbs 4:23

1917 Lifesaving Bible

The Bible that intercepted shrapnel aimed at German infantryman Kurt Geiler

Late 1800s The Invisible Mother

The long exposure time of early cameras meant creating in-focus photographic portraits of children—prone to fidgeting—was tricky. One common solution? The child sits on the lap of an adult who is covered by a cloth. Later the photographer crops and blurs her out of the picture, leaving the portrait of the child miraculously in focus.

The Old Jokes Are the Best

The sound of laughter has always been the same

The First Finger?

Boston Beaneater Charles Radbourn flips a timeless gesture to the photographer on Major League Baseball's Opening Day. Some suspect that Radbourn is actually holding a cigar, but he made the same unmistakable gesture in the photo on his baseball card.

1800s Animal conga line

ca 1952 Two girls masquerade as lobsters at a Rockland, Maine, Lobster Festival.

1910 Fritzi Massary, actress and operetta singer, in a chicken suit

Late 1880s
Military Photobomb

Everything old is new again,
including photobombs.
If you can't see it, keep looking.

Very many happy returns of the day

Miss Tabbie at the Rink

Rinking at Brighton

The Photographer

Pointers Pets

1870s–1880s Cats Before the Internet

Proving that a) cats have always been intrinsically funny and b) there are riches in niches, English photographer Harry Pointer became well known for the more than 200 picture postcards he sold featuring his pet cats.

Look at those horrid "Brighton Cats" Bull

The Shah

A happy new year

Bring up the dinner Betsy

A happy new year

1891 Marcel Proust, author of the novel *In Search of Lost Time,* plays air guitar on a tennis racket.

GIANT GRASSHOPPER SHOT NEAR MILES CITY MONT.

1937 Joke postcard for tourists showing a legendary "giant grasshopper"

Old-Fashioned Fashion

Achieving the look
was always in style

Beauty Contestants

Graciela Marino (second from right) and other
contestants in the Miss World contest under the dryers

1967 English supermodel Twiggy in a sequin-jumpsuit-hand-thong ensemble

Dress made to be worn at the English royal court

1863 Brighton Swimming Club

One of England's oldest swimming
clubs, the Brighton group was
founded in 1860 as a men's club
for swimming enthusiasts. They swam
and competed at Brighton's beaches.

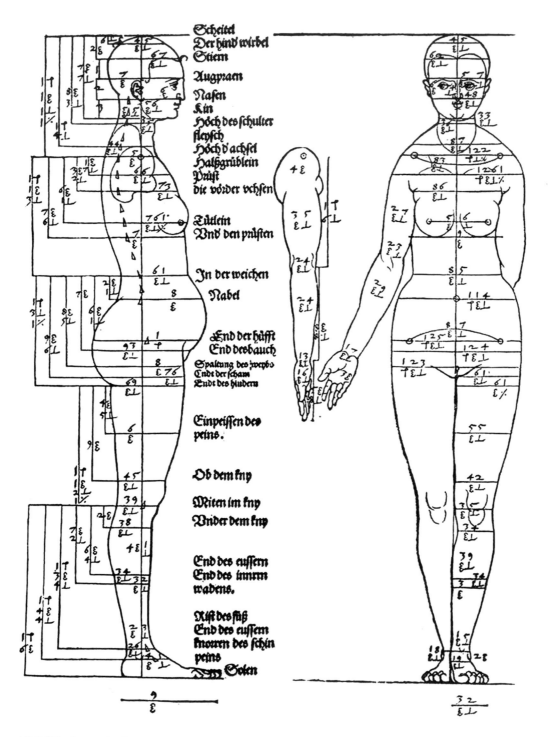

1528 "Studies on the Proportions of the Female Body" by Albrecht Dürer

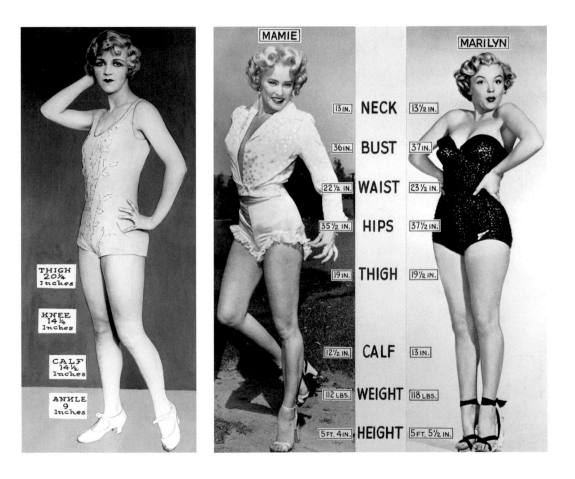

THIGH
20¼
Inches

KNEE
14¼
Inches

CALF
14½
Inches

ANKLE
9
Inches

MAMIE   MARILYN

	MAMIE		MARILYN
NECK	13 IN.		13½ IN.
BUST	36 IN.		37 IN.
WAIST	22½ IN.		23½ IN.
HIPS	35½ IN.		37½ IN.
THIGH	19 IN.		19½ IN.
CALF	12½ IN.		13 IN.
WEIGHT	112 LBS.		118 LBS.
HEIGHT	5 FT. 4 IN.		5 FT. 5½ IN.

1930–1950s The Feminine Physique

Above left: Gladys Turner is the winner of a pretty leg contest in New York. Her "stems" are ideally propor-tioned. Above right: Comparison of American film actresses Mamie Van Doren and Marilyn Monroe.

1968 Actor Richard Harris

Wearing a Nehru jacket of his own design
at the time of his hit single "MacArthur Park,"
Harris is better known today as Professor
Dumbledore in the first two Harry Potter movies.

Early 1900s Men in double-breasted fur coats

ca 1941 Waterproof Makeup

Aquatic performers apply lipstick underwater.

Alternative

Realities

4

Time as a Remix

We often think of the past as if it were written in indelible ink and can't be edited or erased, but maybe it can. What if we saw history from a whole new angle? Could a little-known moment captured on film change everything? What if we were to discover that Alice of *Alice in Wonderland* was real, or that mass murderer Adolf Hitler would take the time to pet a roe deer, as you will see in this chapter?

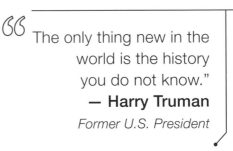

66 The only thing new in the world is the history you do not know."
— **Harry Truman**
Former U.S. President

The past is populated with remixes. There was a time when pop artist Andy Warhol dressed up as a superhero, when elite Japanese women were trained as warriors, and when the dome of the U.S. Capitol building was painted communist red.

We think we are different from people in the past. But they are us in costume, as they throw medieval snowballs, ride through city streets on scooters, and express their feelings with emoticons. :)

The past refuses to fit our maps, no matter how we stretch them. And if our understanding of the past shapes our understanding of "now," could these new visions of the past help us create a new present?

1800s This elite female warrior, or *onna-bugeisha,* served as her family's protector.

Past & Present Collide

The Old World and the New World touching base

1957 *Mayflower II*

A blimp greets the *Mayflower II* in New York Harbor. A replica of the original *Mayflower*, the *Mayflower II* retraced the historic 17th-century voyage from England to Plymouth, Massachusetts.

1950s Pilots "steered" the VZ-1 Pawnee "Flying Platform" by shifting their body weight.

> "Let me tell you what I think of bicycling. I think it has done more to emancipate women than anything else in the world. I stand and rejoice every time I see a woman ride by on a wheel."
> — **Susan B. Anthony,**
> *woman suffrage pioneer*

ca 1916 Suffragette on a Scooter

Lady Florence Norman got a new "set of wheels" as a birthday present from her husband.

1300s Medieval "Baseball"

This sketch, found in the margin of a 14th-century "book of hours," or calendar, shows a game of "stool ball," or "stump ball"—which bears a striking similarity to baseball.

1800s Victorian pinball machine

TYPOGRAPHICAL ART.

We wish it to be distinctly understood that the letter-press department of this paper is not going to be trampled on by any tyranical crowd of artists in existence. We mean to let the public see that we can lay out, in our own typographical line, all the cartoonists that ever walked. For fear of startling the public we will give only a small specimen of the artistic achievements within our grasp, by way of a first instalment. The following are from Studies in Passions and Emotions. No copyright.

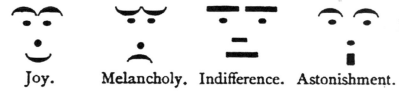

Joy.   Melancholy.   Indifference.   Astonishment.

1931 Pigs crossing Camden Road, London

Egyptian mummies for sale

1910 Twin Deck Phonograph Cross-Fader

The cinematic world was never content with the silence of the
silent-movie age. One solution was to play records, but most
were too short to last through a movie. Enter the chronophone:
A skilled "chronophonist" could cross-fade between two
records, creating a seamless segue, much like an early DJ.

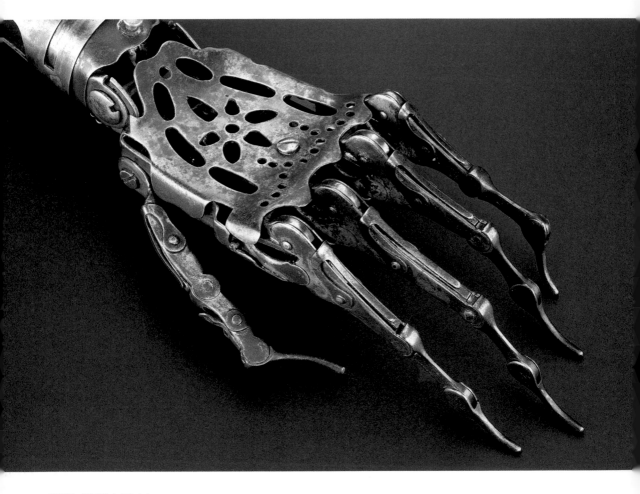

1850–1910 Artificial arm

1974 Polish firefighting monks

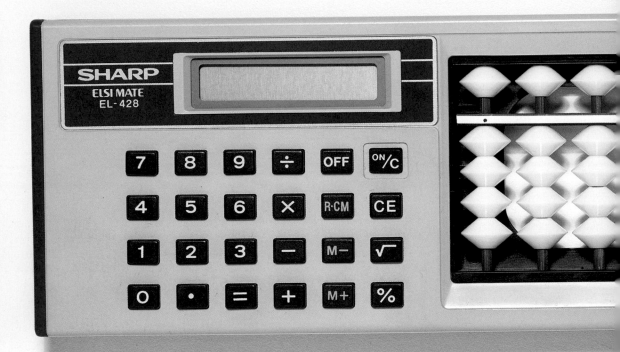

1970s Hybrid Calculator-Abacus

This Japanese device was used temporarily until people switched from the abacus to the calculator. Today, the abacus is still used in many countries as a counting machine, so this hybrid is less an updater than it is a translator between two mathematical worlds.

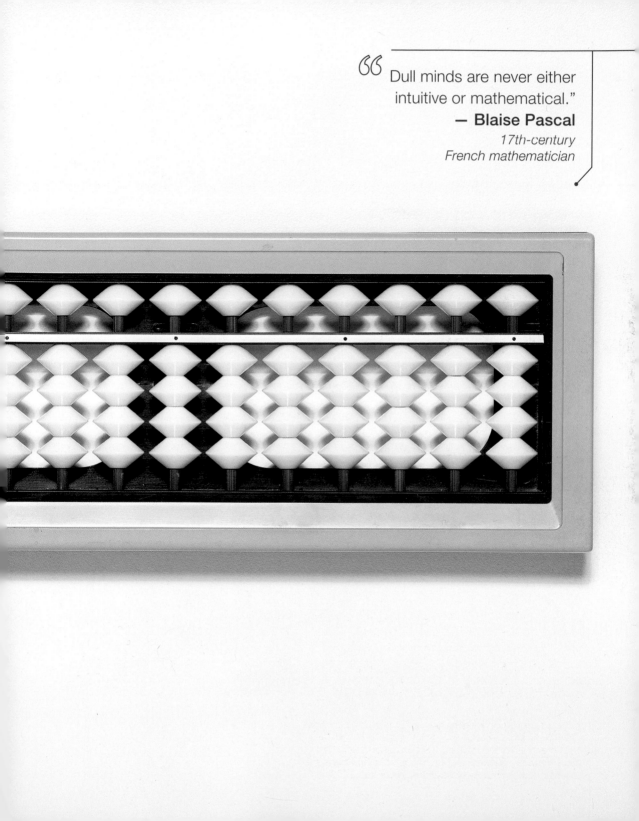

Late 1300s–1407 Medieval Snowball Fight

This timeless detail represents January in the "cycle of the months" frescoes at Buonconsiglio Castle in Trento, Italy.

1400s The infant Jesus in a baby walker, from the prayer book *Hours of Catherine of Cleves*

Parallel Universes

It was almost a different world

1959–1960 **The U.S. Capitol in Red**

The blushing dome is not a sign of a communist takeover.
It's part of a restoration that included coating the dome
with red anti-corrosion paint.

1967 Katharine Hepburn skateboarding

1967 Model/actress/singer Nico and pop artist Andy Warhol as Batman and Robin

1975 Kentucky Fried Chicken, Abu Dhabi, U.A.E.

A cowgirl puts a nickel in an El Paso, Texas, meter where she parks her pony.

mid-1900s Women's History, Afghanistan

Above: A female student in a high school in Kabul (1981).
Opposite: A professor (right) and her students at the Faculty
of Medicine in Kabul examining a cast of a human body part
(1962). The Taliban ended education for girls in the late 1990s.
Now efforts are under way to bring it back.

> 66 The mind is not a vessel that needs filling, but wood that needs igniting."
> — **Plutarch**
> *Greek historian and writer*

ca. 1924 The original "Hollywood" sign, an ad for a real estate development, lost its "land" in 1949.

1860s Women Who Fought as Men in the Civil War

Opposite: Sarah Rosetta Wakeman fought for the Union and died from dysentery. She was buried as a man. Above: Union cavalryman "Jack Williams" (left) was really Frances Clalin (right), who enlisted alongside her husband. She saw battle 18 times and drank, chewed tobacco, smoked cigars, and gambled to fit in.

Gothic Models

The "Gothic" of "American Gothic" refers to the architectural period of the house in the background of the painting, rather than the stern faces of its imagined occupants. Artist Grant Wood imagined his male inhabitant to be a farmer, but the model was in fact Wood's dentist. The woman is Wood's sister. This photo was taken 12 years after Wood painted "American Gothic" in 1930.

Beatrix Potter and her pet rabbit

ca 1862 The Real Alice in Wonderland

Alice Liddell's father was friends with Charles Dodgson, aka future *Alice in Wonderland* writer Lewis Carroll. Dodgson made up the *Wonderland* story to entertain Alice and her sisters. Dodgson gave Alice an early version of the manuscript, called *Alice's Adventures Under Ground,* as a Christmas present.

1940s The real Maria von Trapp (far left) and the Trapp Family Singers creating (the sound of) music

ca **1879** The only known authenticated photograph of outlaw Billy the Kid

King Mongkut, the royal inspiration for the musical *The King and I*

1934 Child star Shirley Temple meets the Shirley Temple doll.

1928 Comic genius Buster Keaton deadpans with a Buster Keaton doll.

Evil Takes a Holiday

Darkness on its day off

1973 Franco Goes Fishing

Spain's General Francisco Franco,
fascist dictator and avid angler

1930 Stalin making faces at his bodyguard

1940s Nazi leader Adolf Hitler playing with a roe deer

> He is killer and clown,
> big-hearted buffoon and
> strutting martinet."
> — *Time* magazine
> *from a 1977 profile*
> *of Idi Amin*

1972 Idi Amin
Playing the Accordion

Up to half a million people died under Idi Amin's
reign as president of Uganda. Known as the
"Lord of All the Beasts of the Earth and Fishes
of the Seas and Conqueror of the British Empire
in Africa in General and Uganda in Particular,"
here he takes a break from conquering to
sound out a tune on a squeeze-box.

1977 Kim Jong Il visiting an amusement park, Pyongyang, North Korea

1938 Italian dictator Benito Mussolini (in the lead) goes jogging with the troops.

The Shock of the Old

Yesterday can be a scary place

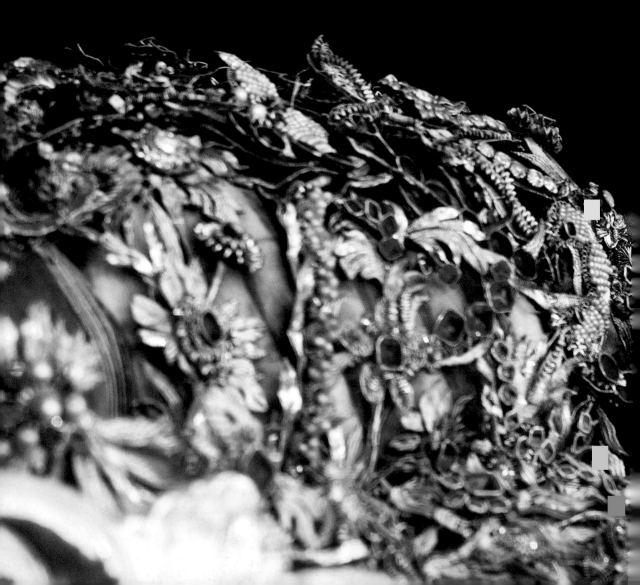

ca 1600s **The Jeweled Skeletons of "Saints"**

To combat the Reformation, the Catholic Church draped ancient skeletons in jewels, proclaiming them the lost relics of early Christian martyr saints. There was little evidence to support the claims.

1876 "Eaten by Mountain Rats," Colorado

Pvt. John O'Keefe, an attendant on Pike's Peak in the Rocky
Mountains, related a dramatic story of huge, man-eating rats
that had attacked his family and devoured his daughter. He
erected the tombstone on the mountain to commemorate her
loss. The news spread, and soon a trail of tourists started traveling to the summit to see the tomb. This trail ended when it was
revealed that O'Keefe had never been married and had no children. He had concocted the story to increase tourism.

British golfer E. A. Smith claimed that he never misses.

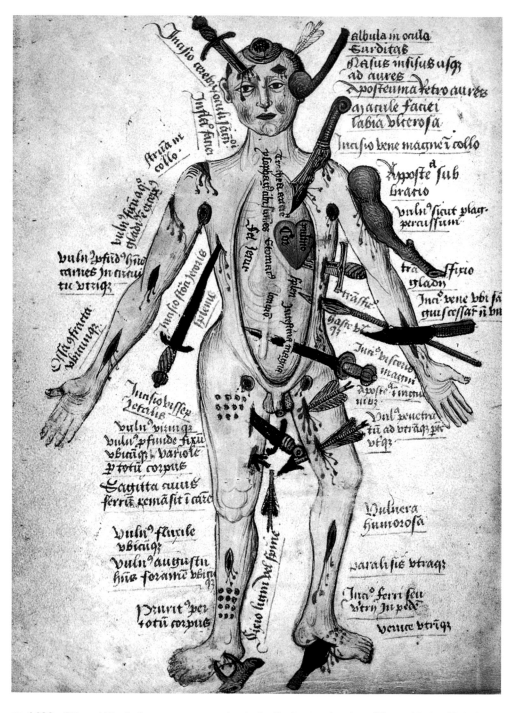

ca 1400s "Wound Man" diagrams were anatomical crib sheets, showing different kinds of injuries.

ca 1490–1500 An allegory of Nature forging a baby

ca 1930s–1950s Violent Valentines

(Clockwise from top left) Nothing says "I love you" like describing yourself as veal, threatening to shoot and/or drown yourself, comparing your valentine to handcuffs, aiming a gun at your valentine, boiling your valentine in a cauldron, suggesting your valentine is a dictator, eating fire, or using your superpowers to spy on your sweetheart.

mid-1800s–early 1900s
"Spirit" Photography

The first "ghost" photos were taken accidentally when people walked through long-exposure shots. Some photographers used the technique to make novelty cards; others claimed to capture spirits on film. Above: Mary Todd Lincoln with the "ghost" of her husband, Abraham Lincoln, ca 1871. Left: A ghost photo, 1920s

1955 Power at Your Fingertips

Electricity flashes from the thimble-topped fingers
of a "preacher-scientist."

1862 Electrotherapy to tone facial muscles

ca 1930 Lioness
on the Wall of Death

Lions were sometimes used to add
an extra element of danger and
excitement at motorcycle racetracks
known as Walls of Death.

It's a Big, Small

World After All

5

Time as Scale

All maps have scale—the size at which we see the map in relation to our world. Our maps of the past are no different. So if we want to see the past differently, we can simply change the scale.

When we zoom in, the zeitgeist of a particular era can be seen in minutiae. And when we zoom out, the smallest details can capture massive historical events in a single picture.

> 66 Who controls the past controls the future; who controls the present controls the past."
> — **Winston**
> *in George Orwell's* 1984

We zoom in on the 1950s, and the world of the atomic bomb is everywhere, from swimwear to toys. We zoom in on 1900, and the American gold rush is more than a concept, it's an endless line of men scaling a treacherous, snow-covered mountainside.

We zoom out from a picture of two American veterans shaking hands in 1913—one from the North and one from the South—and that handshake helps bring closure to the U.S. Civil War. We zoom out from a picture of a former slave sitting in a rocking chair on a porch, and her eyes contain the history of slavery.

And at some point, our maps fade. The border between *now* and *then* breaks down. And stretching out to touch us are these ghosts, offering us close-up and panoramic views of what we thought we knew.

1901 Annie Taylor was the first person in history to go over Niagara Falls in a barrel—and survive.

Normal Nuclear

The everyday world of the atomic

1957 **Nuclear Observers**

These NATO observers look more like spectators at an atomic detonation in Nevada.

1957 The last Miss Atomic Bomb, Lee A. Merlin

1951 Atomic bomb hairdo

1962 The Cuban Missile Crisis

U.S. Army antiaircraft rockets, mounted on launchers and pointed out over the Straits of Florida in Key West, Florida, toward Cuba

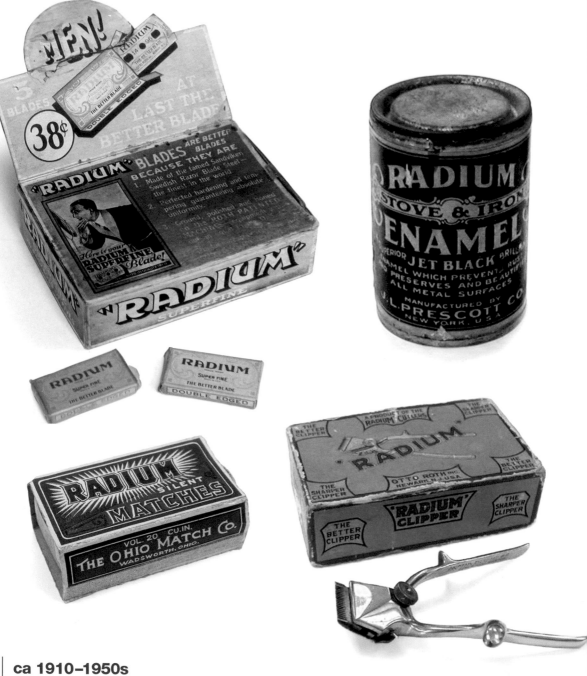

ca 1910–1950s
"Radioactive" Products

During the first half of the 20th century, radiation and its potential power could be used to sell almost any product.

> **RADIUM**, n. A mineral that gives off heat and stimulates the organ that a scientist is a fool with.
> – **Ambrose Bierce**
> *19th-century American writer*

1958 Backyard Bomb Shelters

A new "family-type" bomb shelter on display
in Milwaukee, Wisconsin

1947 Radiation Safety Posters

Produced at Oak Ridge National Laboratory in
Tennessee, these posters introduced personnel to
"Health Physics," or radiation protection.

1946 An underwater atomic bomb test at Bikini Atoll, Marshall Islands, Micronesia

> "Time I am, the great destroyer of the worlds, and I have come here to destroy all people."
> — **Krishna**
> *in the Bhagavad Gita*

It Happened to People Like You and Me

Eyewitnesses to history

Child Miner

Lewis Hine's pictures of child miners changed American law. Above: Vance, 15, earned 75 cents for working a 10-hour day—his sole job was to open and close the door. Because the mine was so dark, the pictures on the wall were not visible until the photo was developed.

1983 Weather Forecaster Auditionees

At one San Francisco TV station, a competition is under way. The prize? The chance to present the weather forecast. These contestants are among the hopefuls.

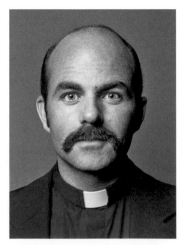

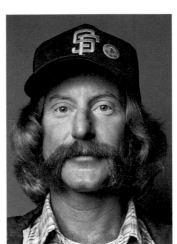

1911 Child oyster shuckers, Mississippi

ca 1900 Prospectors climb the 33-mile (53 km) Chilkoot Pass to the Yukon, Alaska, goldfields.

1932 Marching for Beer

"Beer for Taxation" parade on Fifth Avenue during Prohibition and led by Jimmy Walker, then the mayor of New York City

1974 American Gas Shortage

Above: Locals turned this abandoned Potlatch, Washington, gas station into a religious meeting hall. Right: Parked cars were tempting targets for thieves looking to siphon gas. This father and son sent a clear message: Don't even think about it.

ca 1876 **Deadwood, U.S.A.**

A notorious and lawless gold-mining town in Dakota Territory, Deadwood appeared almost overnight with the discovery of gold in its hills.

1857 Olive Oatman

Kidnapped by Native Americans when she was
14 years old, Olive Oatman was returned to her
family five years later with this facial tattoo.

1913 North meets South: U.S. Civil War veterans from opposite sides shake hands.

1930s Portraits of Former Slaves

From left to right: Green Cumby, Texas;
Andrew Moody and his wife, Tildy, Texas;
Unknown couple; Esther King Casey, Alabama

1968 Watching Robert F. Kennedy's funeral train pass by in Philadelphia, Pennsylvania

1914 Suffragette Surveillance

Above: Using the literal arm of the law, a Scotland
Yard officer restrained suffragette Evelyn Manesta,
forcing her to have her picture taken. Right: Through
the magic of early photo manipulation, the arm
became part of her scarf in the photo released to
the public.

MADE AND COLORED BY
Charlotte M. Pinkerton
874 JACKSON BOULEVARD CHICAGO, ILL.
864

ca 1890s Blackfeet Country

Lantern slides—an early form of slide projection—showing Montana Blackfeet country, including campfires at night (right)

FROM THE STUDIO OF
CHARLOTTE PINKERTON BLAZER
PASADENA, CALIF.

L45

Tearing Up Our Maps

Charting earlier worlds

GREENLAND

ICELAND

Arctic Circle

Faroe I^s
Shetland I^s
Orkney I^s

Edinburgh

NORTH SEA

Newfoundland

FRANCE

R.Loire
R.Garonne

Oporto
Leon

Lisbon
R.Tagus
Tangier
Cadiz
Gibraltar
MOROCCO
Mogadore

ATLANTIC OCEAN

Azores

Madeira I^s.

Canary I^s.
C.Bojador

ALGIERS
Alicant

C.de Gata

BARBARY

Tropi

Lucayo or Bahama
San Salvador
Group

WEST INDIA

Porto Rico
Hispaniola
Cuba
Jamaica
Antigua
Guadaloupe
Montserrat
Marigalante
Dominica
Martinico
Trinidad

ISLANDS

C.Blanco

Cape Verde Isles
C.Verde
R.Senegal
R.Gambia

COAST OF

C.Palmas

Fernando
Princes
I.S.Thomas
Annabon
C.L.

Cape

1830 Discovering America

This map depicts clouds parting at the discovery of America. The clouds enclose the outer edges of the European-known world from the beginning of the division of the Mongol Empire in 1294 (far right) to the early exploration of the Americas, 1492–1498.

Meeting
of the Atlantic
and Pacific
"The Kiss
of the Oceans"

Canal Statistics.
Length . . . . 40 miles
Channel width at top . . . 500 to 1000 ft.
  „   „   „ bottom . . 300 to 650 ft.
Time of passage Through Canal . 10 hours.
  „   „   „ Locks . 3 hours.
Gatun Dam { Length of crest . 8000 ft.
            Extreme width . . 2600 ft.
            Height above normal lake level 80 ft.
Locks { At Gatun . . 3 double sets | Average lift 82 ft.
        „ Pedro Miguel 1 double set | Length . 1000 ft.
        „ Miraflores . 2 double sets | Width . 110 ft
Culebra Cut . . . Length . . . . 9 miles
Total number of men employed 40,000
Estimated total cost 375,000,000
Area of Canal Zone . . . . 448 Sq. Miles

1915 The Kiss of the Oceans

A postcard from the Panama-Pacific International
Exposition symbolizes the Panama Canal's ability to
connect the Atlantic and Pacific Oceans. The canal
opened in 1914.

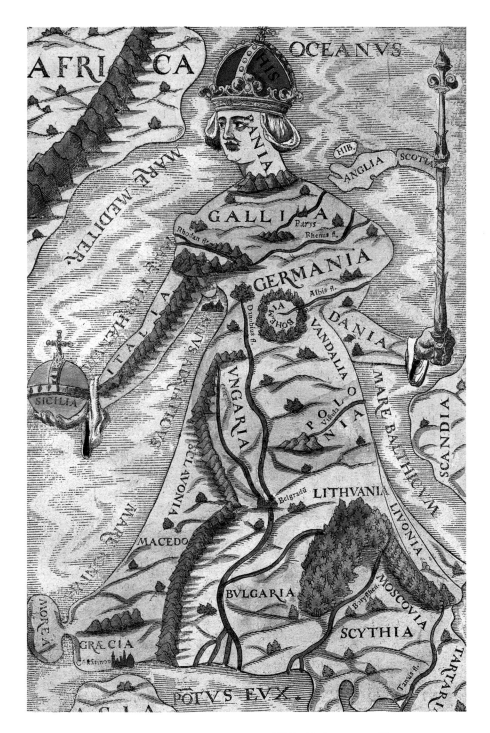

1500s Cartoon map of Europe as queen

1914 Illustration of the
Great European War

This satirical Japanese atlas of the
world features animal personifications
of each country.

This *orbis terrarum* ("globe of the world") organizes the world around the Bible.

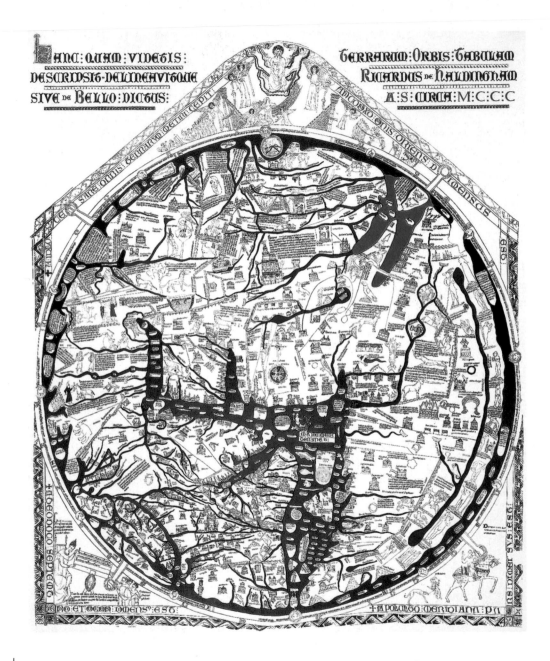

ca 1300 *Mappa Mundi*

The largest medieval map still known to exist, this *mappa mundi* ("map of the world") reflects the prevailing worldview of Christian Europe at that time, with Jerusalem as the spiritual and literal center of the map.

1248 Adam points accusingly at Eve in this world map found in a monastery in Palencia, Spain.

1513 Piri Reis Map

A map compiled by Ottoman admiral and cartographer Piri Reis shows the western shores of Europe and Africa, the Atlantic Ocean, and parts of Central and South America. A note in the margin says it is based on Christopher Columbus's maps, but the explorer's maps were never found. Rotate this page clockwise to see the proper orientation of the map.

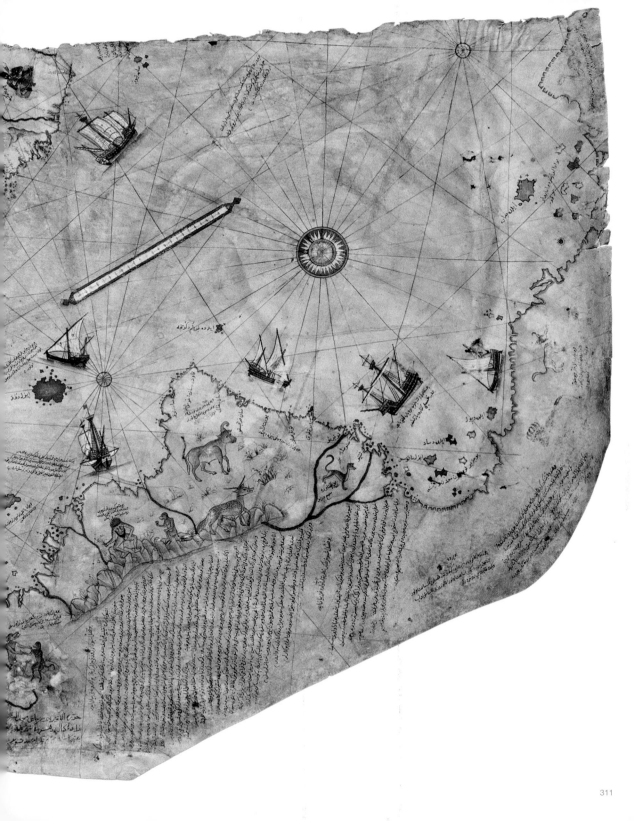

Firsts and Lasts

You have to start somewhere,
you have to stop somewhen

1910 First Airplane Flight From a Ship

Demonstration pilot Eugene Ely takes off from the U.S.S. *Birmingham,* staying airborne for five minutes before landing on a nearby peninsula. His flight marked the beginning of the U.S. Navy's flight program.

ca 1879 The world's first steam-powered submarine, *Resurgam (I Shall Rise Again)*

1899 The First Vehicle to Hit 62 Miles an Hour (100 km/h)

Named "La Jamais Contente" ("The Never Satisfied"), the automobile broke the speed record even though it was an electric vehicle and the aerodynamics of its torpedo shell were obliterated by the protruding driver and undercarriage.

Invented by Gottlieb Daimler and Wilhelm Maybach, the Daimler Reitwagen is equipped with an internal combustion engine and carved almost entirely from wood.

The Vertue of the *COFFEE* Drink.

First publiquely made and sold in England, by *Pasqua Rosee*.

THE Grain or Berry called *Coffee*, groweth upon little Trees, only in the *Deserts of Arabia*.

It is brought from thence, and drunk generally throughout all the Grand Seigniors Dominions.

It is a simple innocent thing, composed into a Drink, by being dryed in an Oven, and ground to Powder, and boiled up with *Spring water*, and about half a pint of it to be drunk, fasting an hour before, and not Eating an hour after, and to be taken as hot as possibly can be endured; the which will never fetch the skin off the mouth, or raise any Blisters, by reason of that Heat.

The Turks drink at meals and other times, is usually *Water*, and their Dyet consists much of *Fruit*, the *Crudities* whereof are very much corrected by this Drink.

T᷑ iality of this Drink is cold and Dry; and though it be a
D   neither *heats*, nor *inflames* more then *hot Posset*.
      th the Orifice of the Stomack, and fortifies the heat with-
      good to help digestion. and therefore of great use to be
      a Clock a   oo   in the morning.
      ens the *Spirits*, and makes the Heart *Lightsome*.
  g   fore Eys, and the better if you hold your Head o-
  , an   ne Steem that way.

It suppresseth Fumes exceedingly, and therefore good against the *Head-ach*, and will very much stop any *Defluxion of Rheums*, that distil from the *Head* upon the *Stomack*, and so prevent and help *Consumptions*, and the *Cough of the Lungs*.

It is excellent to prevent and cure the *Dropsy, Gout*, and *Scurvy*.

It is known by experience to be better then any other Drying Drink for *People in years*, or *Children* that have any *running humors* upon them, as *the Kings Evil*. &c.

It is very good to prevent *Mis-carryings in Child-bearing Women*.

It is a most excellent Remedy against the *Spleen, Hypocondriack Winds*, or the like.

It will prevent *Drowsiness*, and make one fit for busines, if one have occasion to *Watch*; and therefore you are not to Drink of it *after Supper*, unless you intend to be *watchful*, for it will hinder sleep for 3 or 4 hours.

It is observed that in Turkey, where this is generally drunk, that they are not trobled with the Stone, Gout, Dropsie, or Scurvey, and that their skins are exceeding cleer and white.

It is neither *Laxative* nor *Restringent*.

Made and Sold in St. *Michaels Alley* in *Cornhill*, by *Pasqua Rosee*, at the Signe of his own Head.

1652 Handbill for London's first coffee shop

The Winton Motor Carriage

is an accomplished fact.

They are in Actual Use in half a dozen States and their owners are full of enthusiasm.

THEY ARE AVAILABLE on all roads and hills open to common traffic, at from 3 to 20 miles per hour and at a cost of ½ cent per mile.

Variable Speed Hydro-Carbon Motor. simple in construction

Price $1,000. *No Agents.* and free from odor. 👉 *Send for Catalogue.*

THE WINTON MOTOR CARRIAGE CO., Cleveland, Ohio.

1898 The first automobile ad

319

ca 1838 First Photograph of a Human

You are not looking at a photograph of an empty street (Boulevard du Temple, Paris), but rather a bustling street crammed with people and horses, carts and carriages, all moving at speed utterly beyond the capacity of Louis Daguerre's camera to record. With an exposure time of several minutes, the camera blurs the traffic and all people out of existence—except for the man accidentally photographed while having his boots shined (bottom left).

1903 Finish line of the first Tour De France

1891–1893 Hawaii's last monarch, Queen Liliʻuokalani, was forced to cede her throne to the U.S. in 1893.

1977 Elvis's Last Vacation

In March, Elvis traveled to Hawaii with friends, including Shirley Dieu (right). Elvis died on August 16, 1977.

ca 1858 Last Veterans
of the Napoleonic Wars

These are the men who fought for, and alongside,
Napoleon, in the Imperial Guard. Each sports the
uniform he had marched in some 40 years before.
These photos were taken at an annual veterans
gathering, commemorating the anniversary of
Napoleon's death on May 5, 1821.

> " I'd like to say 'thank you' on behalf
> of the group and ourselves and
> I hope that we passed the audition."
> — **John Lennon**
> *closing line of the Beatles' rooftop
> concert on January 30, 1969—
> their final public performance*

1969 The Beatles' last photo session

Opening the National Geographic Vaults

The World Prepares to Meet King Tut

This photo was taken just before archaeologist Howard Carter entered the inner chamber of Tutankhamun's shrine for the first time. The doors are bolted and tied, with an intact clay seal, proof that grave robbers had not breached this shrine since it was sealed in the 14th century B.C.

A Retronaut Comes Home

One Tuesday evening in 2013, the 43-year-old me got an email from National Geographic.

It wasn't the first time that a publisher had approached *Retronaut* about creating a book, and I'd had a range of conversations with some excellent publishing houses. But that email closed all other conversations.

National Geographic intuitively understands the language of pictures. It is a language they have been speaking through their magazine since January 1905, and I would argue that they have created the greatest photographic archive in the world.

In January 2014, I visited National Geographic in Washington, D.C., and it was there, in the depths of their underground stacks, that I saw an original Autochrome for the first time. The Autochrome was the first commercially available color photographic process, patented by the Lumière brothers. Brought to the market in 1907, the images are made—improbably and delightfully—from potato starch.

After four years of sharing "time-disruptive" photographs on Retronaut.com—and hunting them down in secondhand stores for many years before that—standing among possibly the greatest collection of photography in the world was, for me, to come home.

Here are a very, very few of the incredible pictures I have seen in National Geographic's archive that capture the essence of *Retronaut*.

> 66 Use pictures, and plenty of them."
> — **Alexander Graham Bell**
> *on the inclusion of photography in* National Geographic *magazine*

1988 Guatemalan highland elder 13 years after he appeared in *National Geographic* magazine

1903 Alexander Graham Bell

The National Geographic Society's second
president, Bell, and his wife, Mabel, kissing in
a tetrahedral kite that Bell designed

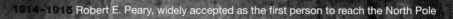

1914–1915 Robert E. Peary, widely accepted as the first person to reach the North Pole

ca 1950 Porters transport a car on long poles across a stream in Nepal.

1919 National Geographic's float at the International Festival of Peace on Independence Day in Washington, D.C.

1903 Unidentified members of the Ziegler Polar Expedition (1903–1905) in the Barents Sea, Arctic Ocean

ca 1955 Dinosaur Country

Tourists ride horses past a life-size *Apatosaurus* statue in Dinosaur Park, near Rapid City, South Dakota.

1965 A face from Abu Simbel temples, Egypt

ca 1912 A Japanese woman plays a samisen.

ca 1954 Folk dancer in Biarritz, France

ca 1948 Costumed clowns and their trick dog

ca 1962 Man checking the antenna on a mock-up of the Telstar communications satellite, New Jersey

1969 Astronauts Under Quarantine

President Nixon (right) and Apollo 8 astronaut Frank Borman (left) greet the Apollo 11 astronauts Michael Collins, Neil Armstrong, and Buzz Aldrin in the Mobile Quarantine Facility (MQF) following their return from the moon. The crew was quarantined for 65 hours, until NASA scientists determined the astronauts were not carrying "moon germs."

1965 Standing Guard

A fainter doesn't faze these guards
in London, England.

Acknowledgments

I would like to thank the following people: Mike Aston, Neil Bates, Chris Batt, James Bilefield, Matthew Brown, Stephen Bodger, Eammon Boylan, Rachel Brickley, Matt Butson, Matt Cannon, Julian Carter, Dan Catt, Tim Closs, Adam Critchley, Sally Duckworth, Bruce Edwards, James Fraser, Peter Gardner, Jack Gavigan, Andrew Gordon, Martha Hawes, Linda Hewett, Elisabeth Hoff, Isabel Hughes, Wiebe de Jager, Christopher Jenkins, Thomas Jones, Chris Lethbridge, Chris Lewis, John Lloyd, Robert Loch, Greg Lockwood, Francisco Lorca, Duncan Mackay, Emily Meritt, Keith Merrin, Nawsty Mitten, Toby Moores, John Nichol, Steve Pankhurst, Bo Pedersen, Victoria Pirie, John Pollock, Milena Popova, Robert Popper, JP Rangaswami, Steven Riley, Liz Ritson, Sara Rowe, Rachel Searle, Lance Thackeray, Chris Thorpe, Harry Verwayen, Anton Wellenreiter, Annie Wild, Catherine Wild, Ian Wild, Ruby Wild, Zebedee Wild, Matt Willsmore, Bruce Woolley. An additional thanks goes to American Classics, Endell Street, Covent Garden, London, England.

Illustrations Credits

Front cover: (dinosaur) Bates Littlehales/National Geographic Creative; (car) Darin Schnabel © 2013 Courtesy of RM Auctions; (Elvis) Photo by Rex/REX USA (1832476e); (goggles) Courtesy Nannini Italian Eyewear (www.nannini. com); (Farrah Fawcett) The Farrah Fawcett Foundation, Beverly Hills, CA/ABC Photo Archives via Getty Images; (eye miniature) Sarah Nehama; (shipwreck) Library of Congress Prints and Photographs Division, LC-DIG-ppmsc-01752; (child with crocodile) John Drysdale; spine: Courtesy Nannini Italian Eyewear (www.nannini.com); back cover: Top (David Bowie) Denis O'Regan/Getty Images; (smokers) Everett Collection/Shutterstock; (Wonder Woman) Photo by Everett Collection/REX USA (287343n); (electricity) Moody Bible Institute/National Geographic Creative; (hair salon) Albert Moldvay/National Geographic Creative; author photo, Elisabeth Hoff.

1 (Goggles repeated throughout the book), Courtesy Nannini Italian Eyewear (www.nannini.com); 2-3, Wikipedia; 4, *Sports Illustrated*/Getty Images; 6-7, Look and Learn/Peter Jackson Collection; 8-9, Bettmann/Corbis; 10-11, Star Wars © & ™ Lucasfilm Ltd., courtesy of Lucasfilm Ltd.; 13, B. Anthony Stewart; 19, Compuserve/NGS Archives; 20-21, Lyndon B. Johnson Presidential Library and Museum; 22 (UP), Michael Furman; 22 (CTR), Darin Schnabel © 2013 Courtesy of RM; 22 (LO), Michael Furman for Ralph Lauren; 23, Mirrorpix/Courtesy Everett Collection; 24, NGS Archives; 25, Sam Hood/State Library of New South Wales; 26-27, Rainer W. Schlegelmilch/Getty Images; 28, Italdesign Giugiaro Archive; 29 (UP), Courtesy Steve Pereira; 29 (CTR), Cheryl Ridge; 29 (LO), © Citroën Communication/Georges Guyot; 30-31, Museum of Flight/Corbis; 32, Fox Photos/Hulton Archive/Getty Images; 33, Fox Photos/Hulton Archive/Getty Images; 34-35, Pip Barnard/Victoria and Albert Museum; 36, Rue des Archives/The Granger Collection, NYC—All rights reserved; 37, Courtesy of Special Collections Research Center/Syracuse University Libraries; 38-39, Cal Acord; 40, Kenneth E. Behring Center, National Museum of American History, Smithsonian Institution; 41, Robert Clark/National Geographic Creative; 42-43, Courtesy of Sotheby's Picture Library; 44, Kenneth E. Behring Center, National Museum of American History, Smithsonian Institution; 45, Courtesy of CapturedWorlds .com; 46-47, NASA/National Geographic Creative; 48-49, NASA; 50, David Pollack/Corbis; 51, Michael Nicholson/Corbis; 52, NASA/Ames Research Center; 53 (all), NASA/Ames Research Center; 54, ITAR-TASS Photo Agency/The Granger Collection, NYC—All rights reserved; 55, NASA/MCT via Getty Images; 56-57, NASA; 58, NASA; 59, NASA/Ames Research Center; 60-61, Advertising Archive/Courtesy Everett Collection; 62, akg-images/The Image Works; 63, R Schultz Collection/The Image Works; 64 (all), fantaisiesbergeret.free.fr; 65 (all), fantaisiesbergeret.free.fr; 66, Advertising Archive/Courtesy Everett Collection; 67, Heritage Image Partnership Ltd/Alamy; 68-69, Takato Marui/Wikipedia; 70-71, Advertising Archive/Courtesy Everett Collection; 72 (all): Wikipedia; 73 (all), Wikipedia; 77, Courtesy Martha Stewart; 78-79, TS Productions/Hulton Archive/Getty Images; 80, U.S. Navy, Official Photograph; 81,